Astronaut's Name

____

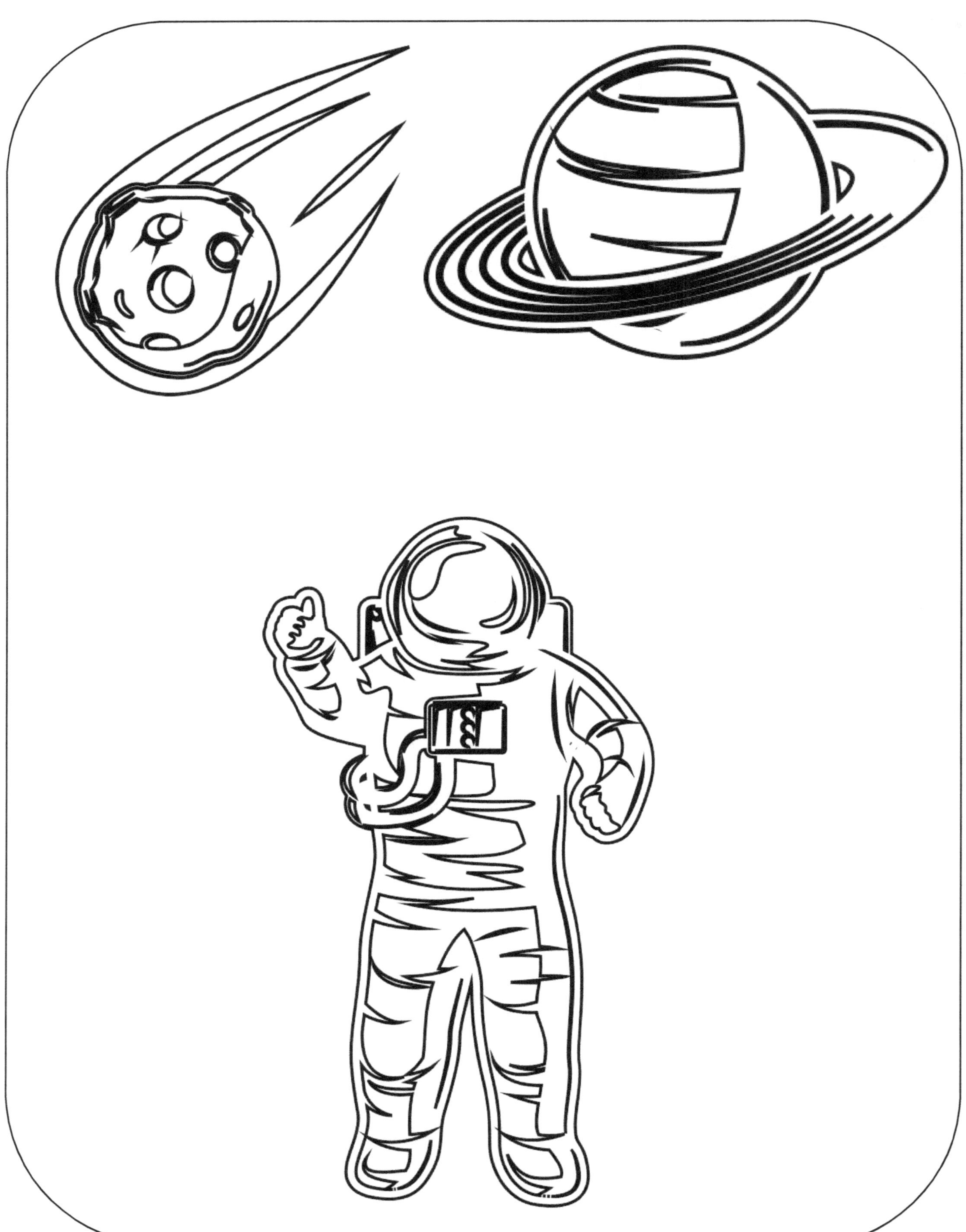

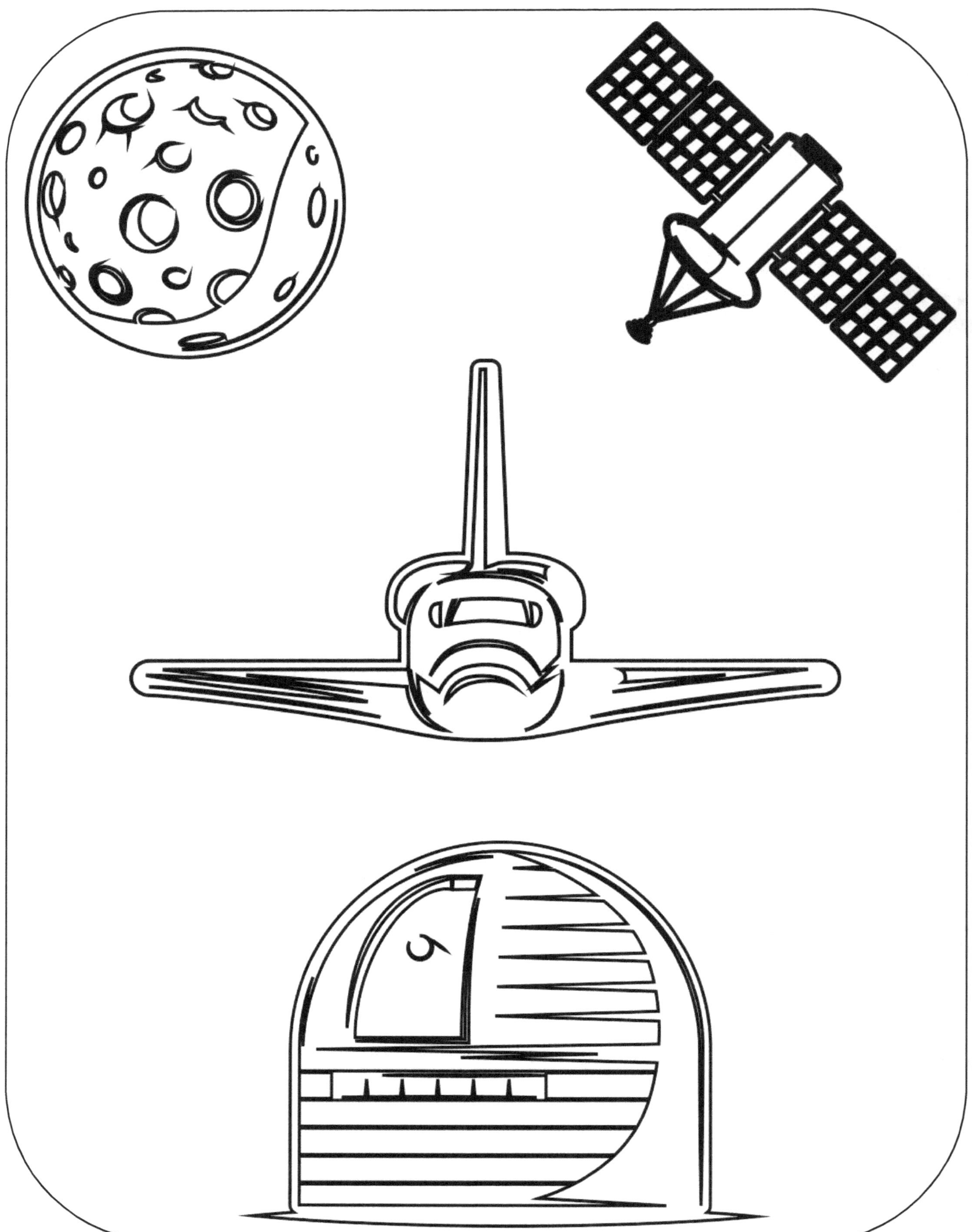

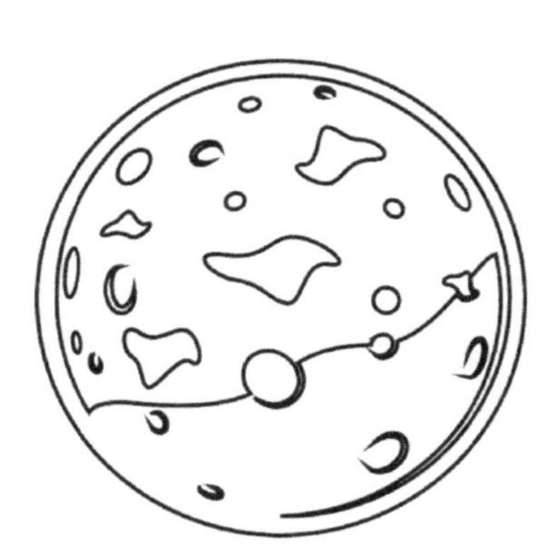
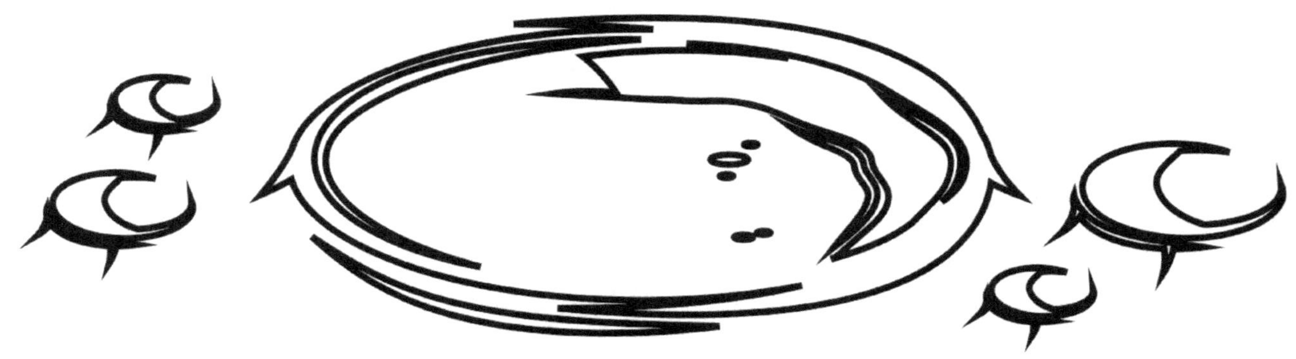

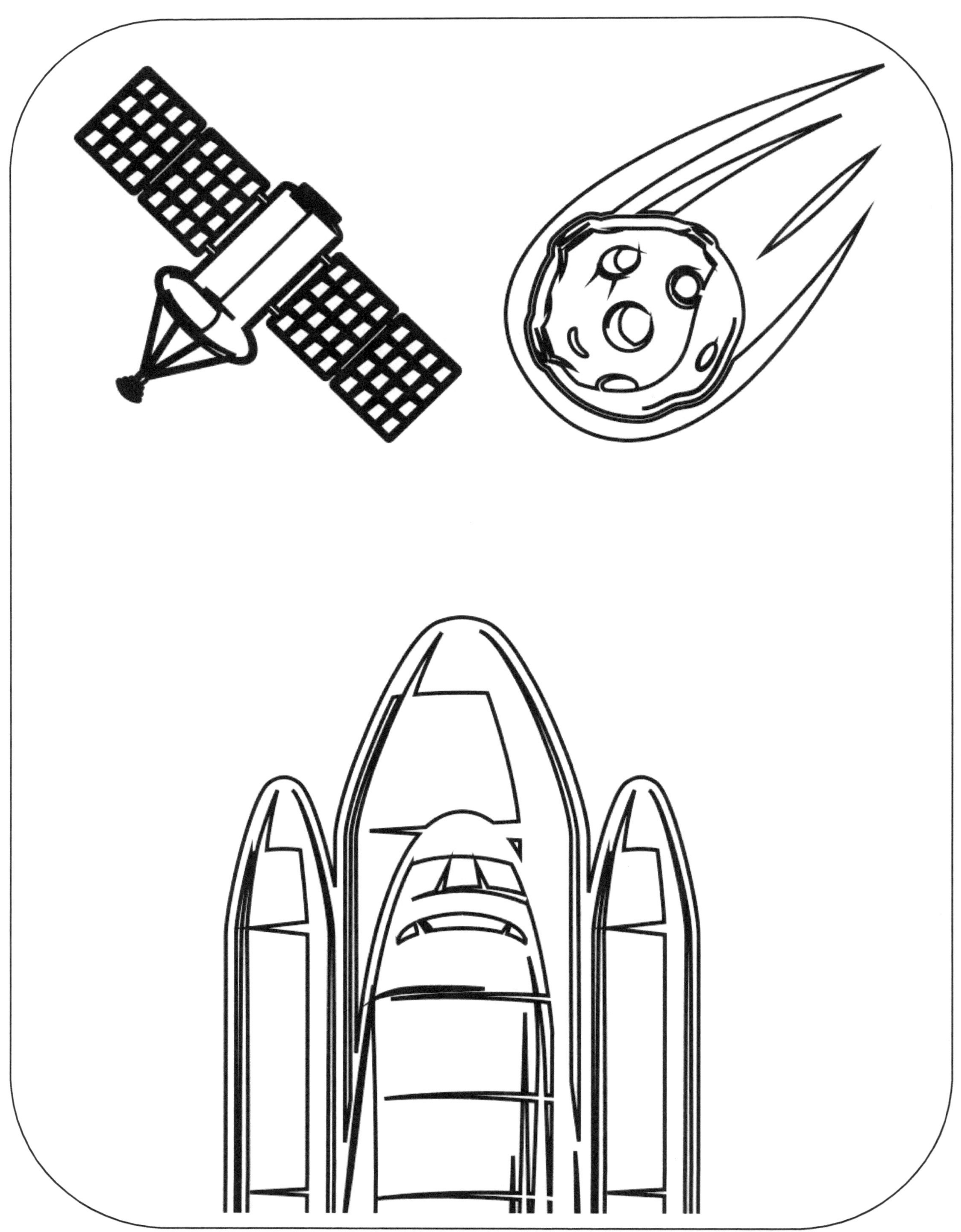

I NEED MORE SPACE

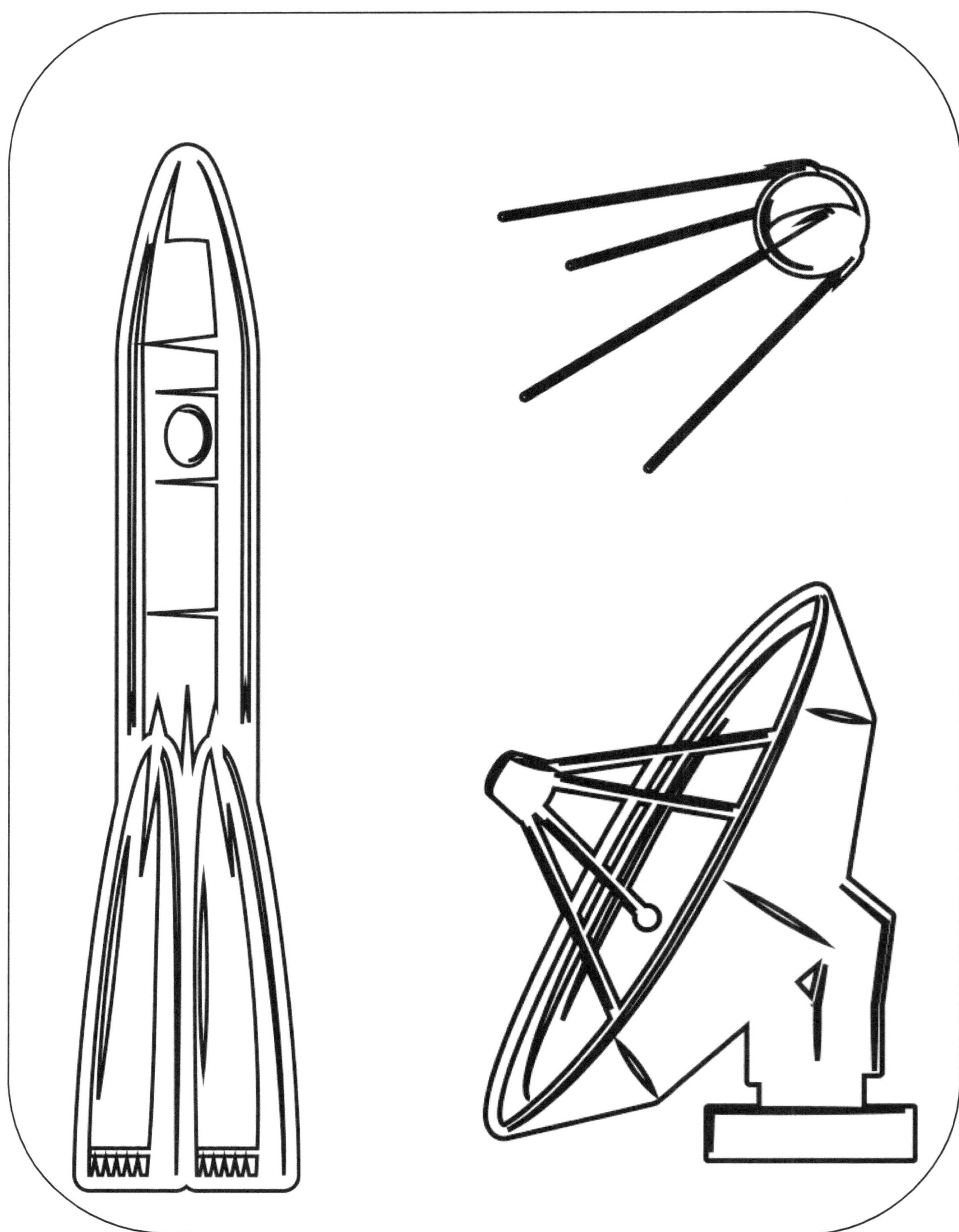

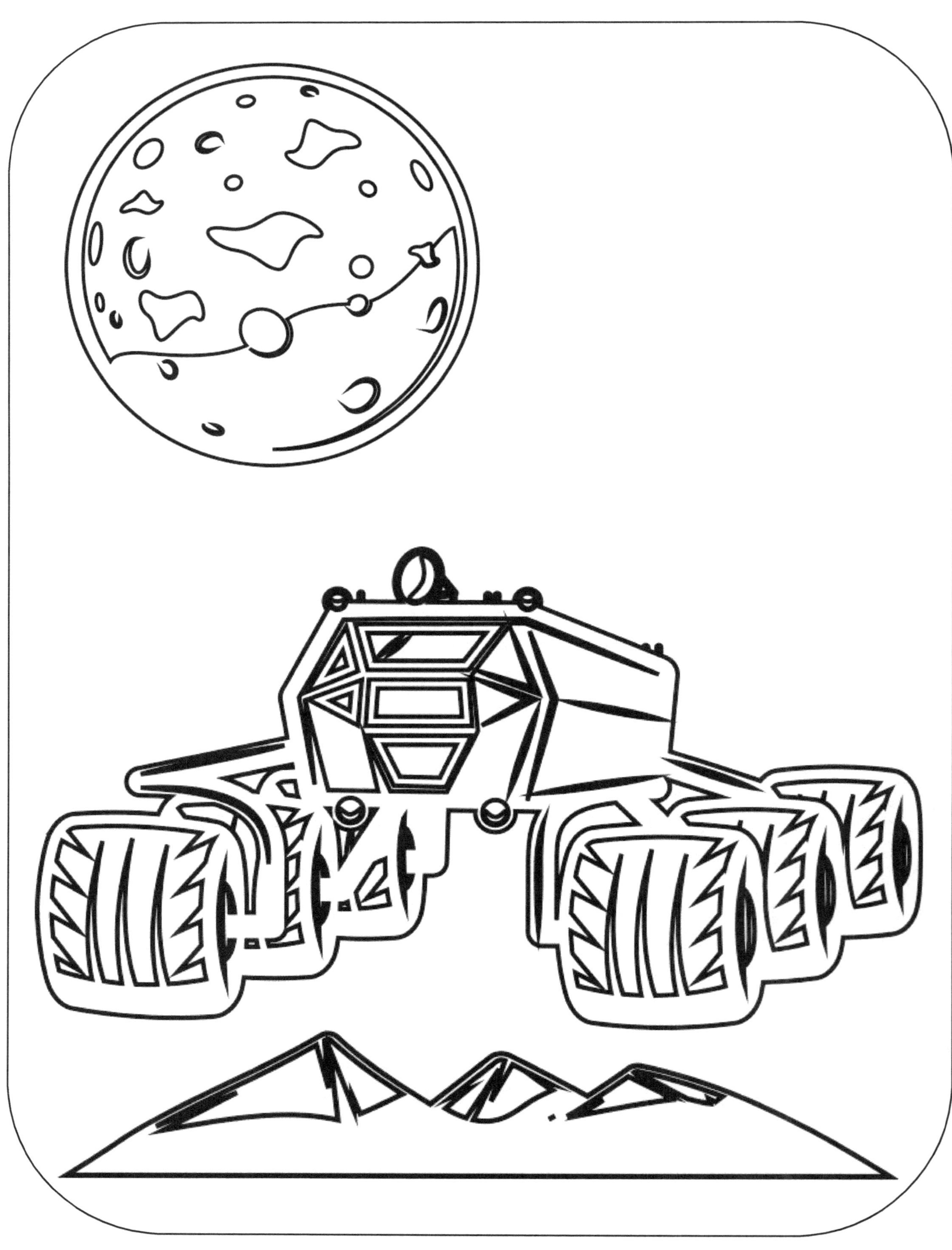

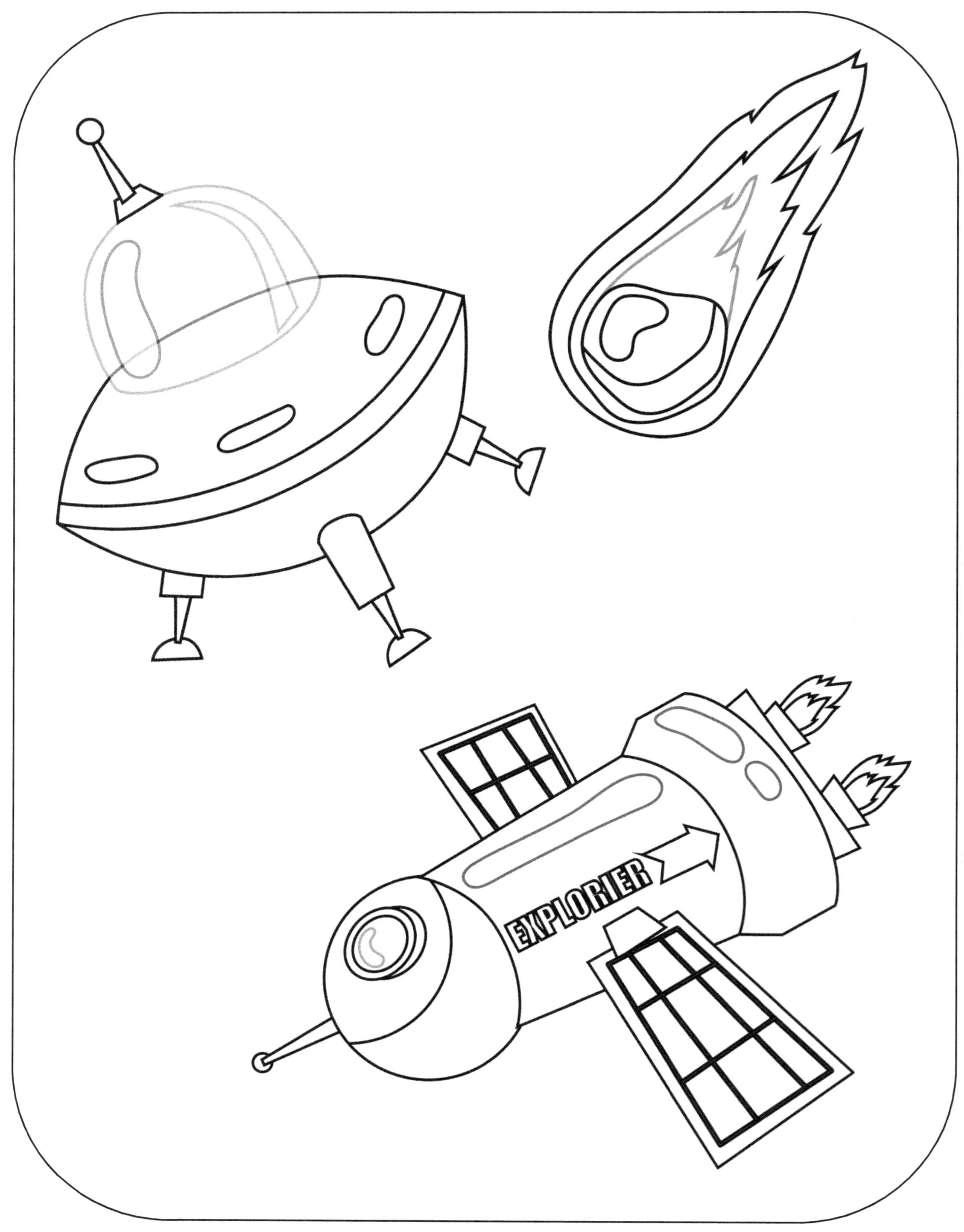
EXPLORER

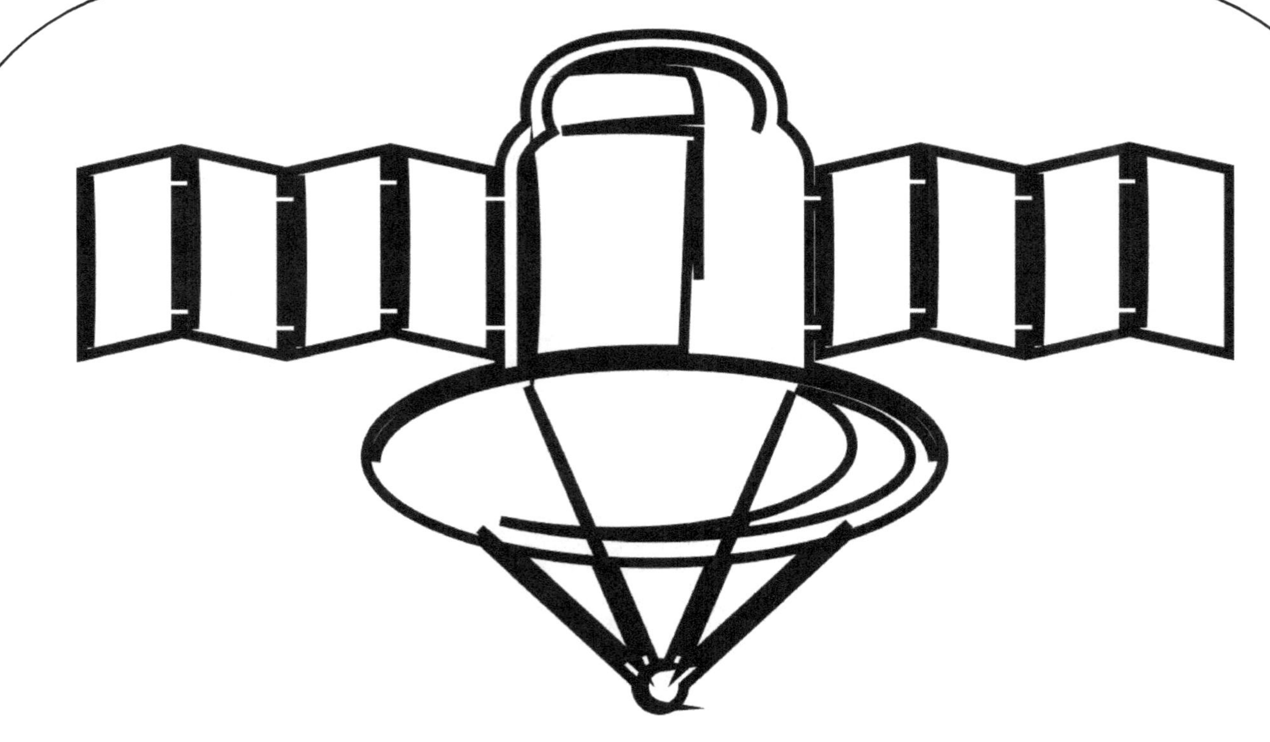

SPACE

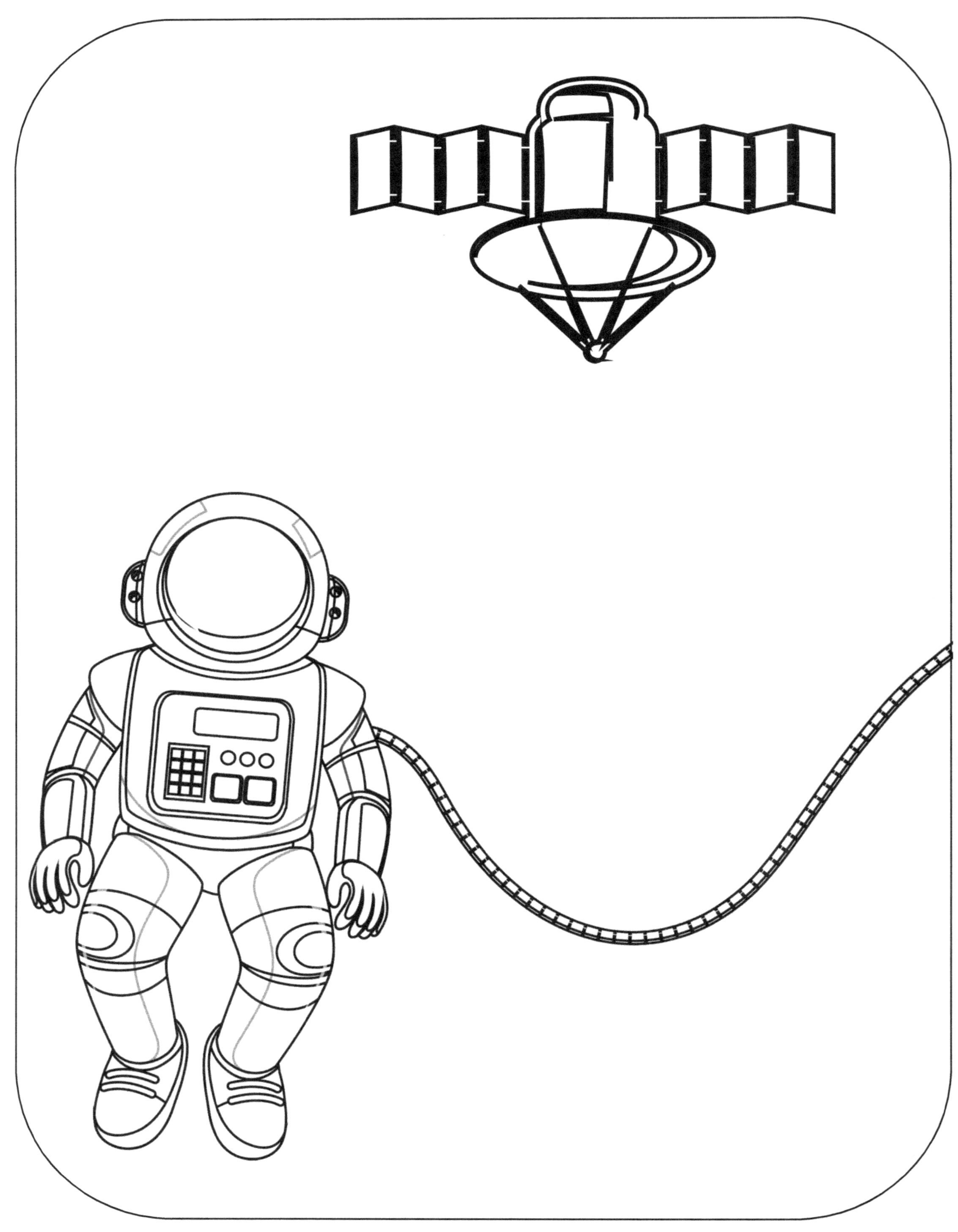

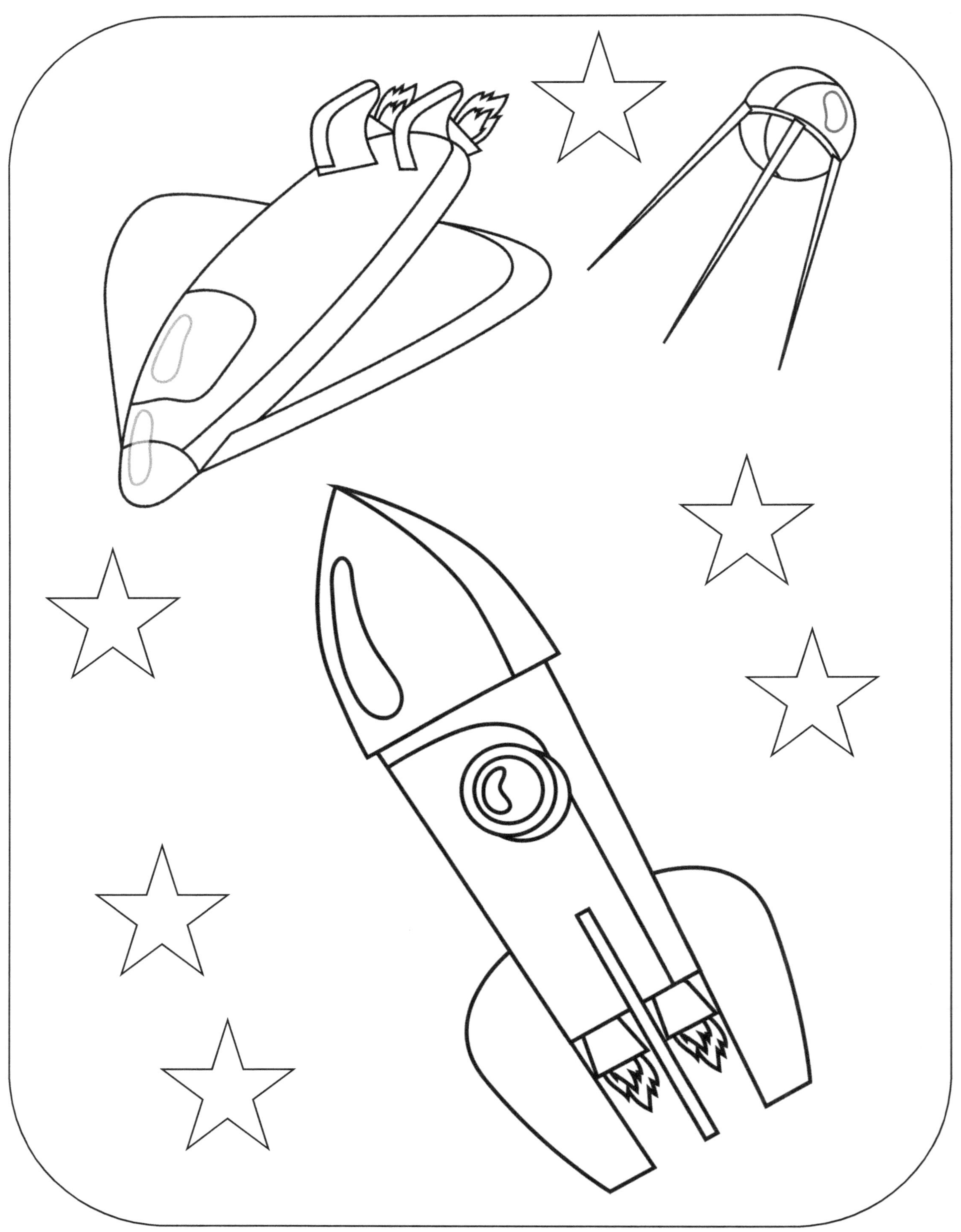

SPACE

Mercury
Venus
Earth
Mars
Jupiter
Saturn
Uranus
Neptune
Pluto
Moon
Sun
Galaxy
Telescope
Rocket
Moon-robot
Satellite

SPACE

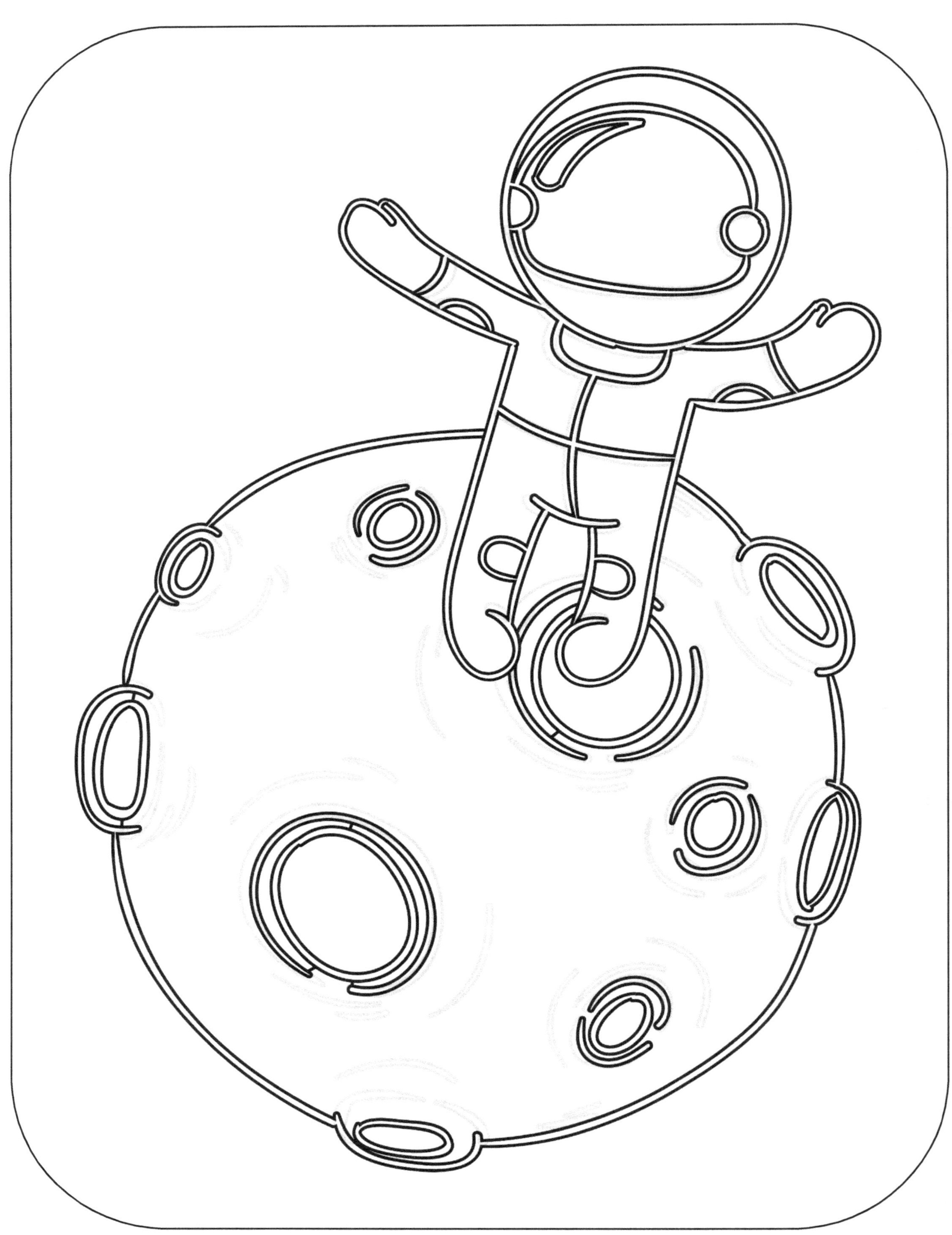